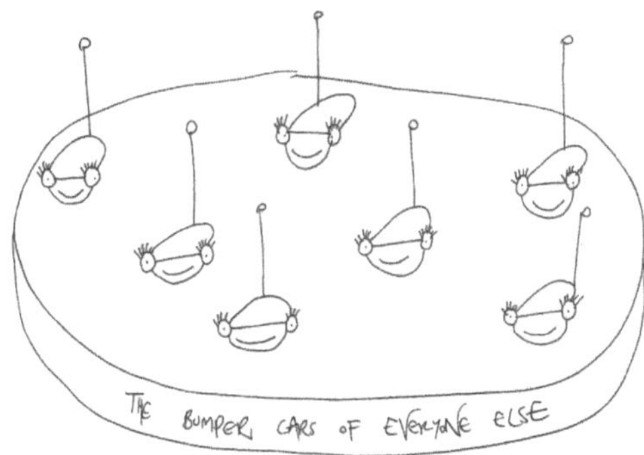

We keep memories of what we looked like in photograph albums … But where do we keep the memories of what we were thinking at the time? Please keep your thoughts in these books as if they were your own journals. Or cut them up and sticky tape them into something else, to keep memories of your mind forevermore.

CLARE-ROSE
TREVELYAN
YONGHO MOON

THE ONE THING & ANOTHERS
Young Philosophers

CLARE
WHY IN THE
WORLD
ARE WE
HERE?

CLARE-ROSE TREVELYAN

Illustrated by YONGHO MOON

THE BOOK WITH NO STORY

Young Philosophers Series Vol. 1
A Collection of Creatures

RedWoolEditions

Young
Philosophers
RedWoolEditions

What happens beyond the universe?

Can I make mistakes and still be alright?

What do I not want to learn?

What do you think about when you are going to sleep?

Why do people want to become famous?

Do you look after yourself?

How should we live our lives and why? These are
amongst the most enchanting questions of all
eternity.

I find the vivid spectrum of answers to these types
of questions more dazzling than a lone colour.
It's through this bouquet of creatures, through the
beauty in the mind of the other, that I hope to get
you thinking and wondering about thinking
and wondering …

HOW TO USE THIS BOOK

❶ Pick any of the 52 creatures.

❷ Read about the particular way they think in the world and think about how we all think differently in our own lives. You may want to ponder the idea of 'diversity of thought' and in what ways how we all think impacts each other like BUMPER CARS in a theme park. Keep all your thoughts somewhere.

❸ Go to the back of the book to make your own thinking creature in a unique outside world.

❹ Create as many creatures as you like, you may be surprised at how your own particular thoughts and the thoughts of other people you know find their way into your creatures. And, if you are lucky, you may discover that it is our inside stories that indeed shape our outside stories and vice versa.

CREATURE PROFILES

These are creatures from my journals, but they have decided that my stories were too boring. They have run away and are looking for children to weave them into new stories of their own.

Fig . 5 .

THE CREATURES

Kasperwish

Kasperwish spends most of his time trying to figure out why on earth he loves everyone as much as he does. He is in awe of everyone he has ever met, regardless of arguments, fundamental disagreements, past actions and mistakes. But why? Was it because he traced everyone's every action through the years to a single intention of love? Was all the chaos that enveloped the world merely just billions of acts of love colliding? And therefore, hate was only found in the brief explosion of the collision? He decided to take a job fixing vending machines while he continued to think.

Persetelephone

Persetelephone is an incandescent mother who takes care of wandering renegades, moon-struck orphans and anxious harbingers on her farm, way out past the east border. She teaches her guests to cook with blue-belles, find strangers in the stranger meadows and swim the rhythm of the short-lived afternoonlia. She goes missing from time to time, occasionally for days on end. Her guests look all over the estate for her but they can never find her. Her silk-sock drawers stay full with splashing memories of all the words spoken to her, from those whose lives she has saved & those who found their afternoons.

Anjelayla

Young Philosophers

T_U
Upper control limit
Central line
Lower control limit
T_L

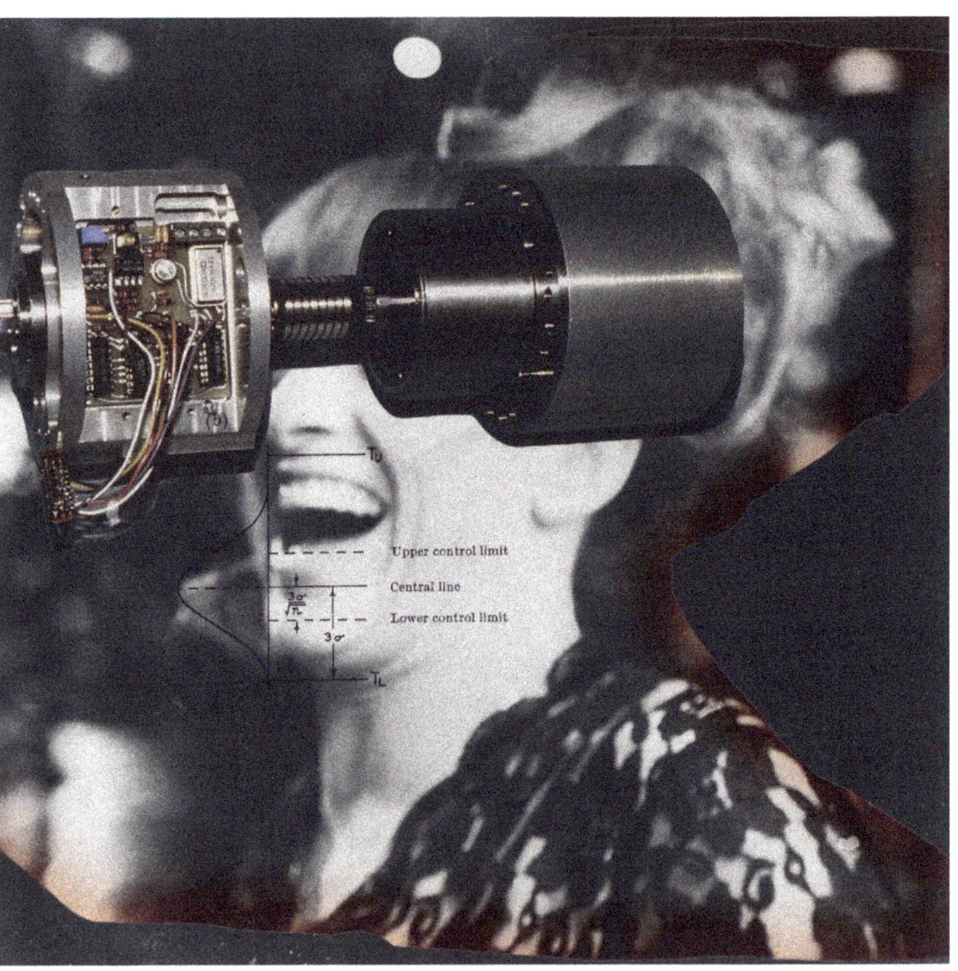

Wanting to throw a party, Anjelayla could not decide whether to celebrate 'similarity' or 'difference'. Is it better to know in our hearts, she thought, that we are all the same? Or to truly accept and celebrate our differences? She was still thinking as she fell asleep, but her thoughts morphed into a littered staircase of glittery orange stockings wielding karaoke instructions. She was calmed by the warming of something that made perfect sense and so she decided she would just throw parties all the time for every reason.

Rupert

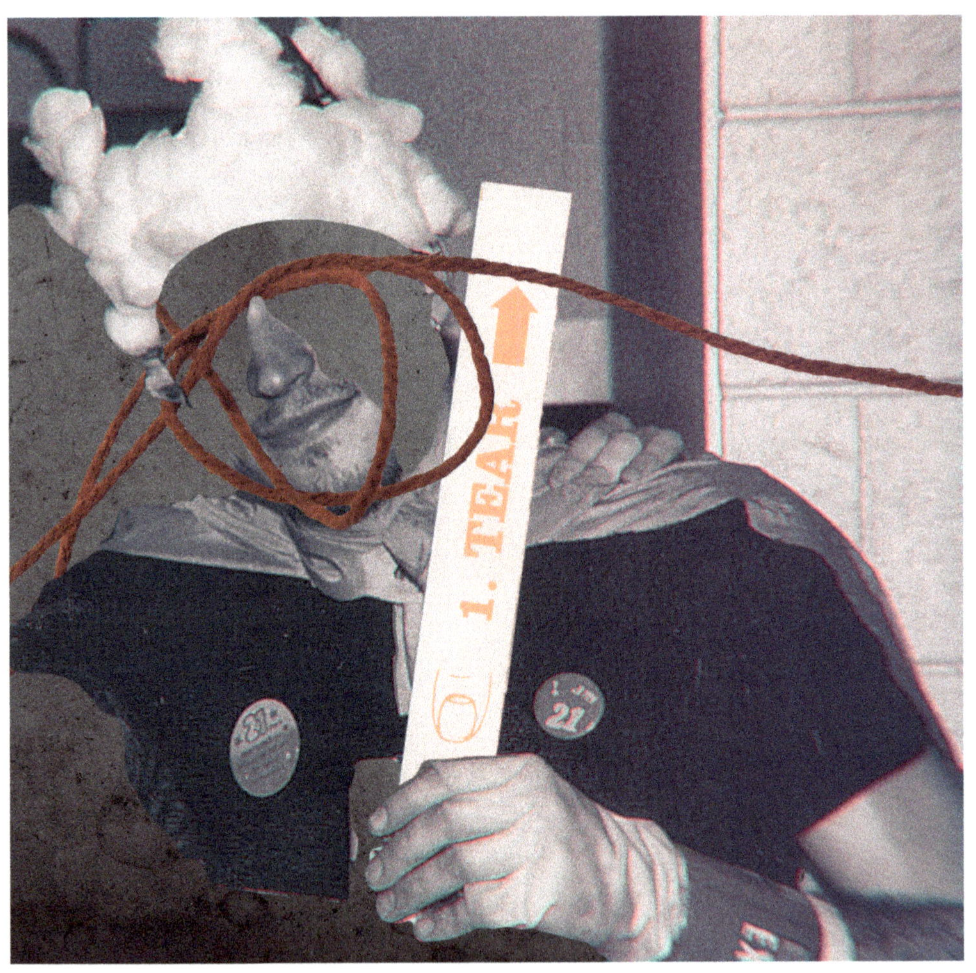

Rupert finds criticising others very natural and so pursued a career in it. He sails with the don't-let-them-see-us-try crowd who mistake their cowardice for intelligence. As a result, he slashes away at life so gracefully he could have been a ballerina. He loves to walk the streets and is often found in altercations with strangers over the most mundane matters. He was very successful back in the day when power was still going to those who stopped at nothing to get it. Now he hides his maps inside magazines when in foreign cities, so no one will ever suspect he's lost his way.

Donnie

onnie fixes peoples cars for free during the night. He sneaks into their carparks and teaches himself all about engines in the process. One night he was thinking about how much he detested the phrase 'having it all.' Even overhearing the words on the street soon became enough to set his temper right off. He believes one can 'live it all', but preferably 'bit by bit'. Sometimes love, sometimes adventure, sometimes success, but not all at once. Oh no. And as for the word 'have'. Hmpf. He simply cannot think of an uglier term to associate with 'it all.' He wants to be a tour guide when he grows old.

Emile

pon discovering that there was not just one truth, Emile stormed home in a fit of rage and threw all his furniture off the balcony. Off went the art deco vase, followed by the neon pink woven baskets, the celery container and then the haunted armchair.

It went on and on until everything was gone. Sitting in the empty bedroom on the polished concrete floor, his friends swarmed around his head crying and screaming, blaming themselves for Emile's anger and his newly acquired nothingness. Eventually they all sat down at various places against the skirting boards and started singing a song none of them had ever heard before, called 'Inside-Out-Choices'. By the time the song was over, Emile wanted his armchair back.

Telescoppy

Telescoppy weaves lace & coriander shoelaces in a small store on Inside-Out street for those who can't breathe too deeply. She watches her customers with great care and wonders if they hide things in the places their breath won't go. Telescoppy's shop is opposite a trumpet and saxophone supermarket. The supermarket has so many more customers than she does because they trick people into thinking what they *breathe out* is more musical than what they *breathe in*. She sleeps in cathedrals and is working hard on her private research project to prove infinity on both sides of her skin.

Rio Gold

By the age of twenty three, Rio was bored. Bored with breakfast, bored with work and bored with sleeping. The boredom slowly began to taint her feelings, and a general sense of gloom came over her. To make things seem better, she would sit on her window ledge and start to imagine the end of the world and other such disasters. She would imagine her boyfriend leaving her, her friends forgetting who she was and losing all her photographs. She imagined getting lost in wilderness with only a compass and a spirit who would follow her, but never talk to her. When she awoke from these daydreams, normal life seemed not so bad after all, and then she could go about her day without the gloom. But she never thought that her thoughts had so much power. By allowing these unwanted situations into her mind so regularly, she was inviting them to stay. And sooner or later, her life started changing.

Joyce Lucinderella

Young Philosophers

oyce was a mind weaving weaponess who lent her thoughts to her father, with footsteps that latched onto the inner most parts of the way he saw life to be. They say she went mad because like all beautiful girls, she thought everyone was treated equally, but by the time she realised that this wasn't the case, the expectations had already infected her heart. She dances still. And sells front doors that open by themselves.

Blind Self

lind was forced to complete question 23 of the personality quiz with a biro-drawn unseen version of himself. He drew a man who couldn't draw. But when he took the blindfold off, the picture was perfect, making it wrong and right at the same time. Colour-synced with the rest of his 22 answers, this same thread of all-ness tangled itself through his answers, and proved he was a truth-teller. Blind decided that he wanted to travel the world for the rest of his life, doing nothing but asking people questions about their story.

Young Philosophers

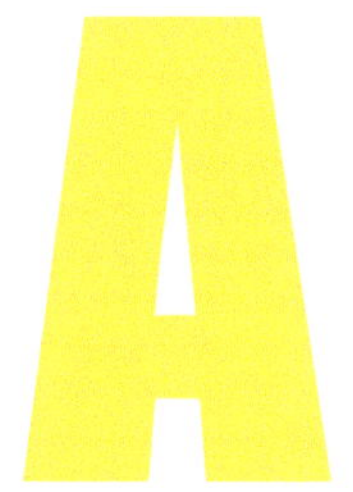

Addition doesn't know what to make. His friend Flyia told him that he'd be happier if he made something, anything. A wall, a soup, a song, a photograph, a pillowcase, a mathematical equation, a policy, a home, whatever he wanted. She guaranteed it would make him feel better, she said it works for everyone. He stood and wondered. Aha. He had it!

He made a story! A story about Flyia.

He gave it to her on a Tuesday.

She hated it.

Addition now works at a bakery and sneakily gives away free bagels to people who are kind enough to ask him how his day has been.

Attachment Smith

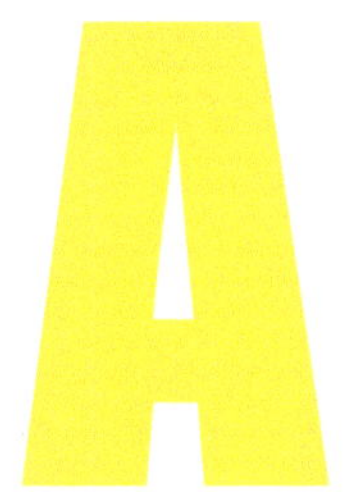

Attachment gets very attached to things, very quickly. So when they inevitably go away and she can't find them, her heart breaks. She sits by her letterbox, day by day, hoping for news of their return. The caterpillars whisper to her, 'everything passes'— she cannot bear the thought, but accepts its truth. But something tip-taps at her mind; she knows everything has an opposite. So if all that we can think of eventually passes, then surely, something must stay the same. But what? She looks for this on the other side of the see-saw and eats the caterpillars in pink. All the while trying to find out what in the world stays the same …

Circles Bizercles

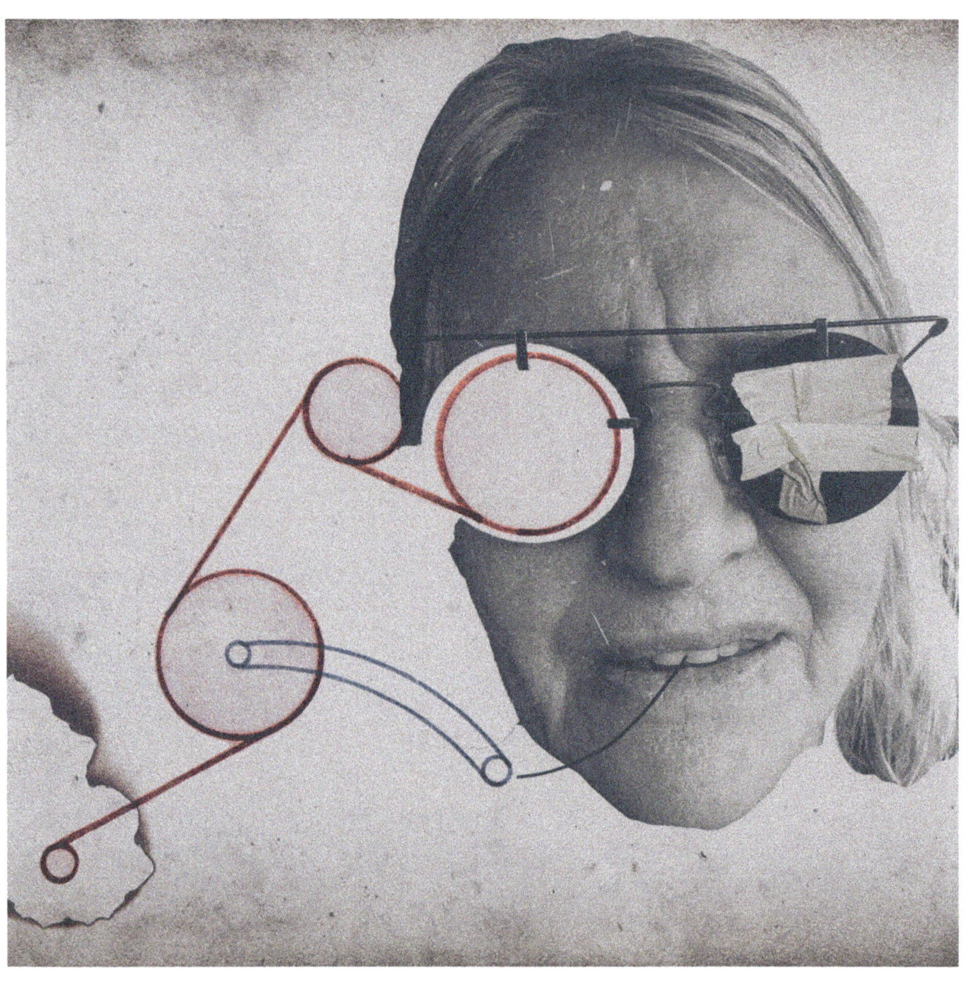

ircles carries dreams from one asleeping person to the next so that all the sleepers can finish each others dreams without their knowing. Circles never knew why she started doing this and sometimes she even questioned whether she should keep doing this.

She awoke from a dream herself just now about thousands of dead butterflies all singing to her in ancient whispers.

"Do what is right, come what may," they sang at various pitches. Shallow yellowness swore itself in tangles upon blue-scream carnies and she knew right away that all she could do was keep going. Heart-led.

Whisperia Matador

Whisperia read something somewhere by someone who said we knew more about outer space than we did about our oceans. Whisperia wondered why we reach further rather than deeper. Maybe it's because we're more scared of what we'll find within. But down where she lives, she knows there is nothing, nothing, nothing but our own spellbinding beauty.

Persephone Bengal

hen Persephone disappears she goes north, piercing the dreamiskya-pockets of those who were cruel yesterday. Not brightly lit explosive cruelness, but the hide-away deniable everyday cruelness. Like the kind of extreme selfishness that swells when the truth is too terrifying.

Or the cruelty that excludes others because they are different. Persephone targets cowards in particular. Puncturing their future-luck with her destiny guns & severing them off from the exquisiteness of knowing those towards whom they are cruel.

Gordon

And now Gordon has lost his luck because silly Penelope has blasted his dreamiskya-pocket with eating-caterpillar bullets. He didn't mean to be cruel to Bruce yesterday. He just was trying to make Bruce be more like him. He merely wanted to Gordonise Bruce. Bruce would make a fine Gordon, Gordon believed. And the more Gordons Gordon had around him, agreeing with him, encouraging him and helping him to Gordonise others, the less likely that he would ever have to change. See Gordon wasn't nasty. He just didn't want to handle the troublesome task of ever, ever, ever having to change.

TaTa La-King

TaTa is the most successful, miserable and intelligent of all the theatre owners in the Kaleidoscope district. TaTa's constant barrage of insulting remarks about other people could just as easily been spat at the mirror. Her secretary, Percival, finds it quite beautiful that this seemingly obvious characteristic is completely lost on TaTa altogether. TaTa also hates eating breakfast food at breakfast. She would much rather gnocchi or roast leeks.

Que Pearlionessa

Que Pearlionessa is missing. She was last seen hatching a plan to break into the haunted palace on the far side of the distant cliff tops. So the story goes that when she crept into the last room, an ancient office, she found a pile of photographs on a large mahogany desk. Pictures of herself in places she had never been with people she had never met. The last photo was a portrait of her in that exact ancient office, standing by the mahogany desk, holding a thousand photographs, silently screaming.

Powderscar Power

owderscar loved power. She even called her first mouse Power. She loved power so much that she was only comfortable when every-thing was under her control. As time went by though, she lost her friends and family. Even complete strangers knew to stay away from her. She had no idea, that if she let go of some of her power, she would still have some. In her mind, to let go of 1% would leave her with 0%. She never was very good at mathematics. But she really loved making salsa and she still is a killer joke teller.

De Fea

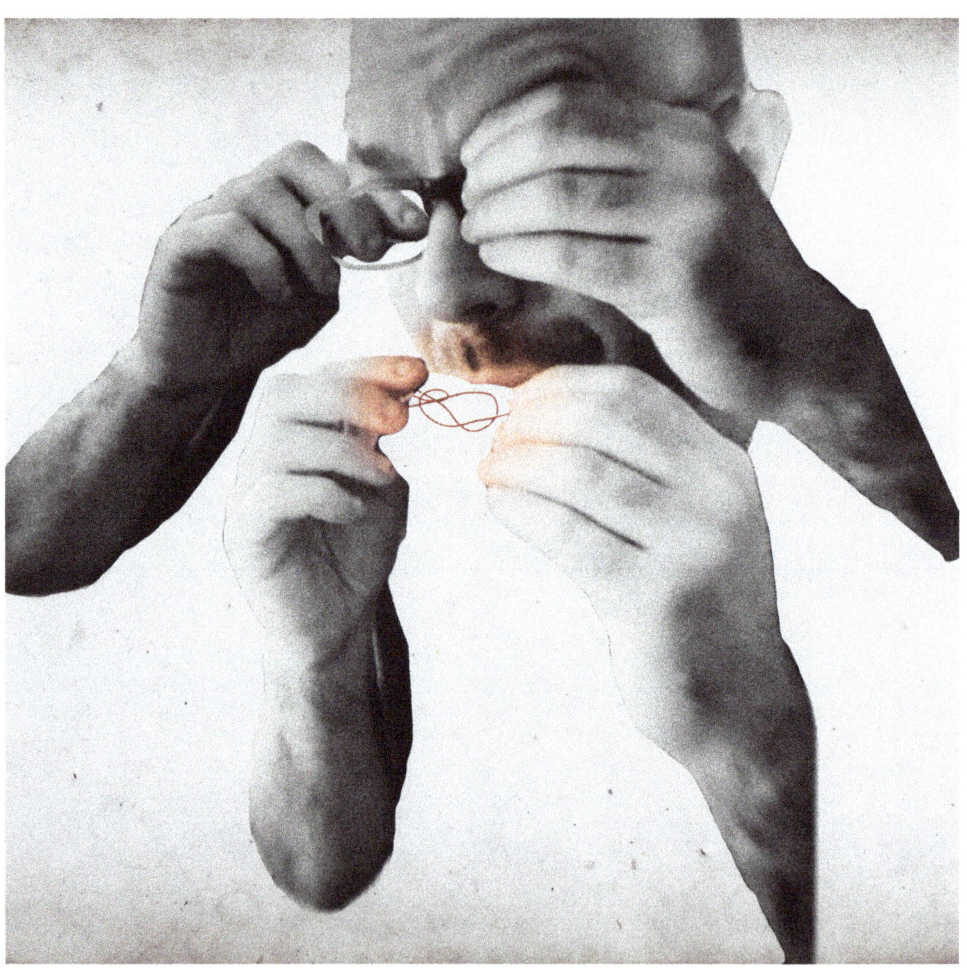

e kept on falling in love with people he wanted to be, not people he could in any way love. This made him miserable. But after years of trying to become happy, he realised that misery too had its perks. And so he stayed miserable.

Once & Challisylis

Once & Challisylis went around their days falling in love with all the different ways of living life. This posed a great problem, for one day they had no idea what to do, what lifestyle to live and who to do it with. Because absolutely everything made sense. They were stuck.

Justincino DeBac

G "Grow up," they said to Justincino. "But how?" Justincino asked. The room fell silent. Then everyone spoke at once. Now Justincino has a list of 886 things to do in order to grow up, and none of them look particularly worth it to him. He may just decide to stay the same.

Mr Mist

The thing about honesty that really annoyed Mr Mist, was that every time he told someone the truth, he lost their trust.

Frederick Penzance

Young Philosophers

Frederick is still trying to figure out how a radio works, while strongly doubting that scientists have finally proven how bees fly. He sure as hell thinks chemicals are natural and he knows, deep down, that everything can be classified as an 'act of god'. Above all else, he believes no one has any idea what they're really doing. He frequently goes to flower nurseries just to switch all the seedling tags around.

Cascadiah

ascadiah has an enemy she hardly speaks of. She and her enemy never realise that they want the exact same thing, and that it is this fact that makes them equals and not enemies.

Jealick

Jealick has a knack of getting really jealous. He cuts off ties with anyone he gets jealous of. Successful? Blocked. On holiday? Blocked. Healthy? Blocked. Can play the cello? Blocked. Jealick also detests complainers. Can't stand them. Tired? Blocked. Moping? Blocked. Heartbroken? Blocked. He wants to live in a hut in the middle of nowhere but in the meantime he runs a ghost and mystery bookshop.

Jaspia Iguana

Jaspia knew happiness was dull from the minute she saw it. It was fraught with warning signs. She remembered back to her great pain, and how it had catapulted her across oceans. The force to overcome her giant feelings was neither distraction nor costume, just mathematics. Worlds intertwined with gangster-witch-riddle-heads and poppy-eyed-truth-sayers kissed her memories with the way the ivy crept around her ankles. So if you are in great pain, she will tell you not to worry. You may be on the tip-toe cusp of your great adventure, like a sling shot that knows how to let itself go.

Writerkychia

Writerkychia was a writer who was thinking about quitting her job. Her problem was this : If she didn't write the exact truth, then what was the point of writing at all? But then, if she did write the truthy-truth of all truth, then it could surely bring her world to its knees, everyone would hate her and then what would be the point of living? She took to drawing. But it tended to knot even more. In the end she thought it was better to live the story instead of wasting any more time trying to tell it.

Gatwick

Gatwick builds mirror mazes. She wants every hallway in the world to be a mirror maze. She can't think of one good reason why this shouldn't be the case. She once got lost after her first heartbreak because when she was being honest, she presumed she was telling the truth.

Rosey

Rosey runs a nursery. She makes so many mistakes in life. So very many. The thing she loves most about mistakes is that no one can make them on purpose. The other thing she loves is her own hypocrisy. She admits that she is most likely hypocritical, but only concedes the point once in a blue moon when she notices it. She likens her hypocrisy to chameleons. She loves chameleons. She has hundreds of chameleons walking around the nursery and sleeping on the flowers. Which is a mistake because not everyone loves chameleons. Another beautiful mistake for Rosey.

Acactux

A cactux loves it when people change their mind: he believes that's as honest as it gets. In his quiet time he trains himself to like the very things he dislikes: like cats, oysters, pea-coats and trapeze artists. When he discovers a particular person he very much dislikes, he will follow that person around as much as he can until he finds something he really likes about them. But that of course tends to annoy the other person, so while Acactux is starting to like them, they are ready to loathe him.

Madga Gaska

Madga Gaska watches out for people who live through several lifetimes. This makes him very wise. He notices that the ones who want control, eventually inspire rebellion in others.

The ones who want fame and adoration are often despised. The ones who cheat their way into too much free time, eventually become trapped in their own make-believe jails. He collects bad art that makes him laugh.

Mrs Stay-Awake

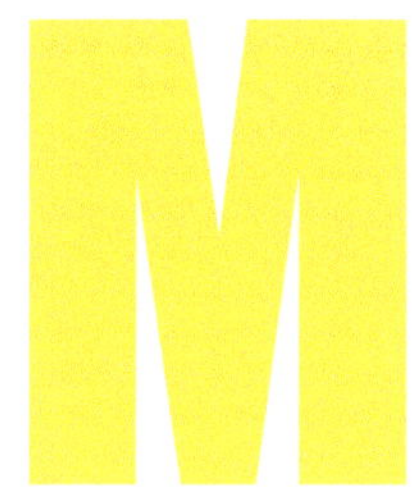rs Stay-Awake is too scared to chase her real dreams. But then she thinks that it's inevitable that the world will blow up one day, and that nothing will mean anything. She then decides that she *may as well* chase her dreams.

But moments later she realises, that for the exact same reason, *she may as well not*. So she still doesn't know what to do with her life. She walks the streets a lot and eventually meets everyone. Your secrets are safe with her because she is bound to forget them.

Habadasha & Jinx

Young Philosophers

abadasha & Jinx are interviewers. They just interviewed 3 billionaires who were pouring a vast amount of cash into scientific research, promising to extend their lifespan and perhaps even eliminate their death. Surely there was another way of living forever? Habadash and Jinx tried to convince the billionaires that they could use their power and generosity to go deeper into living, instead of just elongating life. But the billionaires didn't understand that something so radical could eradicate the very fear they were trying to defeat in the first place.

Death.

Young Philosophers

Bijouxie is a baker who never says a bad word about anyone. This is not because she doesn't notice their so-called flaws but because she reckons that each 'flaw' is actually a 'strength' under different circumstances. For example, her friend Cascadiah is said to be very stubborn, but her stubbornness blossoms into integrity when faced with her ongoing pressures at work. And her other friend Flyia is often said to be very vague. But again, her vagueness also allows her to detach herself from certain things, and so she never tends to overreact. Bijouxie's bread is the best in town.

Pompadompalopogus

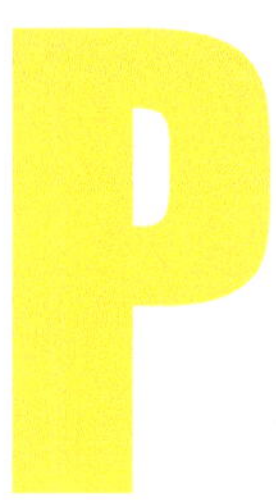ompadompalopogus runs a cafe in the middle of town, directly between the jail and the health club. He never ever talks, he only listens. He has decided that the only thing boring about other people *is what they talk about.*

Yen Yulisp

Yen Yulisp is a gardener who wears blindfolds all the time. The world was so beautiful. But everything in it was temporary. So unfortunately, the world had become too beautiful to look at. Yen sips mixtures of pear and lavender juice while planting new life. She can admit when she is wrong very freely without emotion. This really irritates some people.

Grandfah Gloo

84

Grandfah Gloo worked so hard his entire life so that his grandchildren had the time to wonder, whether what they did in their jobs contributed to the good of society or just satisfied their own egos. Gloo loved to play cards until deep into the night with whomever wanted a game, and he never needed more than four hours sleep. No one ever questioned why he was so happy.

Nighth

Nighth is convinced her favourite emotion is not anger, not sadness, not love, but relief. This proves particularly dangerous because she keeps getting herself into lots of trouble, only to experience the relief of eventually getting out of it. She is unaware though, that the trouble she is getting into is getting thicker and deeper. Tears started to drop from her eyes. But inside the tears, spins a world where mischief is allowed, even on CVs. A casual eye-roll at the glove that twists frightening blueprints of happiness around the throats of sleep-walkers. She is out for the real love.

Drip.

Drop.

Rose

Finally. Rose's two fears had become one. Her fear of death cured her fear of infinity and her fear of infinity cured her fear of death. Now she can finally become the acrobat she has always wanted to be. She just had to run away to find the circus. And on her way through the jungle following the sounds of the ancient circus, she finally understood that she saw what she believed, not the other way around. And there she was all of a sudden, hanging jubilantly from her trapeze.

Charlataniyah

harlataniyah runs a spiritual temple that combines every religion that ever was, with every religion that there is ever going to be as well as some extra made up religions too. Everyone is welcome and his temple is always packed. His biggest belief is forgiveness. He believes everyone should be forgiven for everything because he knows that under any given circumstance, one is constantly getting to know their own brain. But don't be fooled! He will forgive people even if they are mean and horrid, but that doesn't mean he won't secretly go out of his way to also punish them.

Young Philosophers

Oops runs the most popular tavern on all the islands. He always has and he always will. He loves movies and despises people. When a character undergoes a change in a story he cries with pride. When someone claims to have changed in real life he is immediately suspicious and bans them from his tavern.

Whyy & Whyyy

The two mad scientists simply known as Whyy and Whyyy have never left their laboratory. They broke everything down, then broke it down and broke it down and broke it down again. After all this, there before them was the billionth of an atom. And they still knew nothing.

Coyshash

oyshash may have been bullied from time to time in her life, but at the age of 66 she was soaring. Because she knew so well, it was far better to be the one who received the occasional bruises, than be the one who wasted their life throwing the punches. It hurt far less in the long scheme.

Young Philosophers

Capsize and Gallows are madly in love. When they first met me, they had both spent years telling lies to their psychologists but it was getting too expensive. So they fell in love instead and decided to unfold the truth about themselves in a labyrinth so testing and chaotic that they had no choice but to learn to fly out of the maze.

Masqued

Masqued is very bad at perceiving what he's like as a person from another person's perspective. So he can't tell you much about himself at all. He spends 50% of his time staring the grim-knuckled truth dead in the eye and the other 50% of his time pretending it doesn't exist. And when he pretends it doesn't exist, like magic, it doesn't. People who engage in conversation with him automatically talk backwards and think sideways.

Ship & Shap

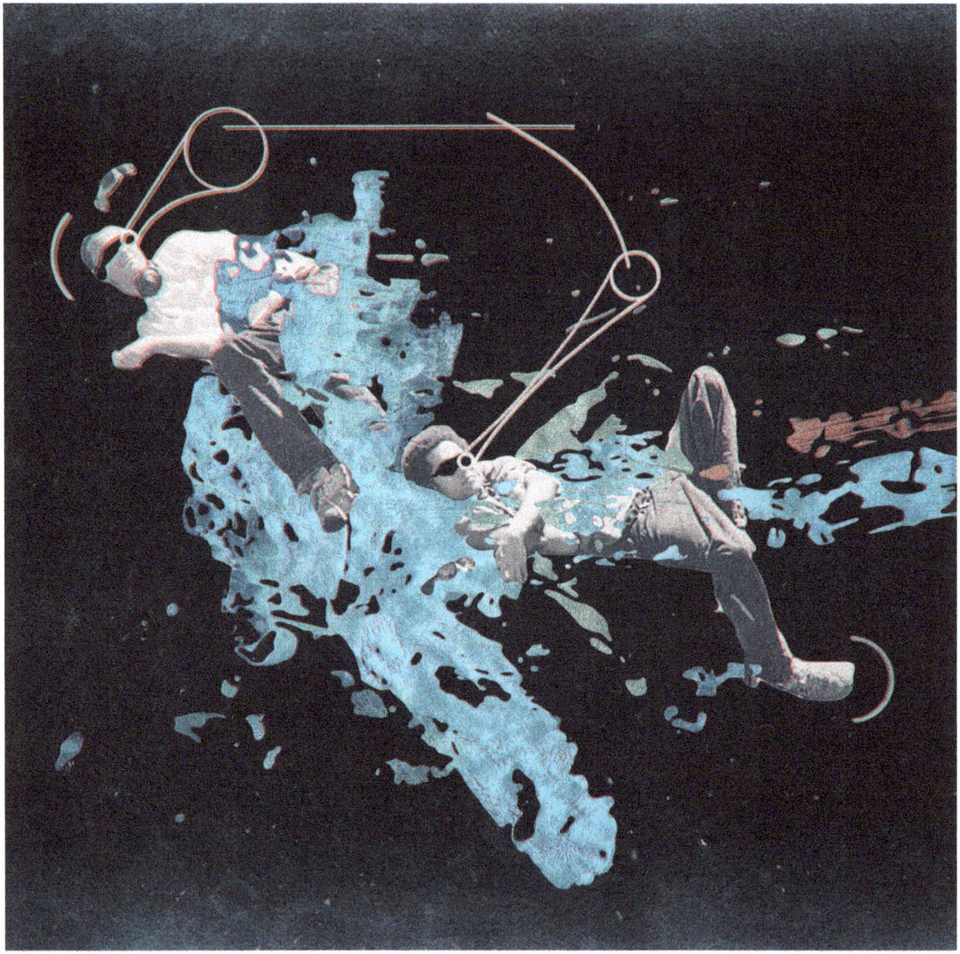

L ike all very good friends who tell
you something not so pleasant
about yourself, they are annoying
when they are wrong and they are
annoying when they are right.

Excellenceee

Excellenceee was a waitress for 7 years before she realised that pretending to work required more effort than actually working. Now she just does the job day in and day out. Her biggest fear is that people will say untrue and callous things about her behind her back. So she makes a big effort to be extra horrible to everyone, because she thinks that if she is extraordinarily nasty to people's faces then nothing worse could be made up about her and said behind her back.

Ponypgijlfas

Ponypgijlfas cares about what other people think, way more than she cares about other people. So she is really nice and yet really mean. But without all the lessons that were on the horizon for Ponypgijlfas to learn, there would be absolutely nothing for her to do. For now, she runs a lifestyle magazine.

Always

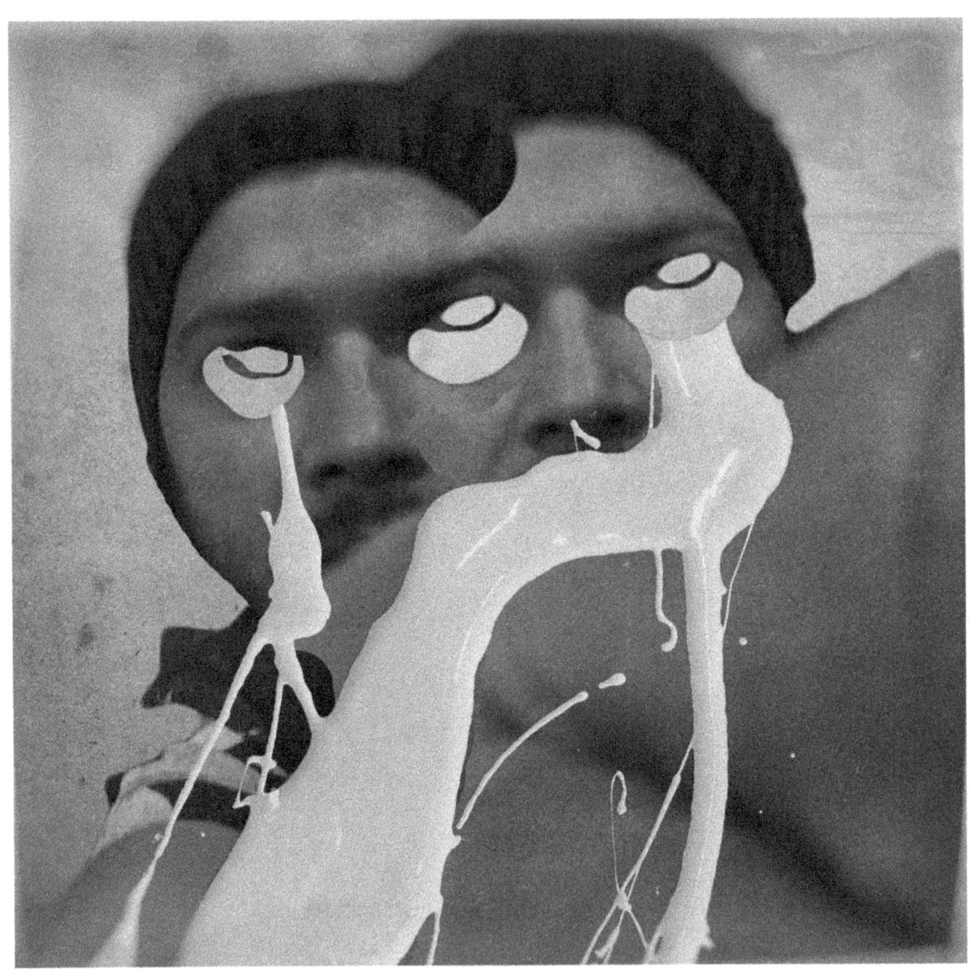

He thinks a thought, then thinks the exact opposite before he decides to run with it or not. But the thing that Always really loves about life, thoughts and choices, is that everything has waaaaaay more than just one opposite. Which means he gets to spend a luxurious amount of his time just lost in his own thinking.

Edie

108

She can't tell if it was the life before or the life after that she got her clues from, it didn't matter. She saw all the signs everyday of her life. The poems in the shadows, the messages in the songs that crept into her hours and the advice that came when two things happened at once. She ran an ice-cream truck her whole life, but that's not how she survived.

Whispa Whispers

Young Philosophers

Throughout my long and spellbinding life, I managed to remember that the love that we gained when we lost what we loved, was often the greatest love that there was.

MAKE YOUR OWN CREATURES

MAKE YOUR OWN CREATURES

Draw them in their world, then ask them a few questions (*Next page*).

What is the most important
thing in their life?

____

What annoys them?

____

What do they do on their birthday?

____

What is their house like?

____

What is their favourite song?

____

What would they change about
the world if they could?

____

What is their favourite type of magic?

____

What is their favourite place to be?

____

Who are their best friends?

____

How do they show love?

____

What do they eat for breakfast?

____

What do they want to do
with their life and why?

____

*What was their biggest mistake
of their life?*

What do they secretly want?

What has been their greatest loss?

What is their biggest fear?

---

*Do they reveal everything they think or
just some things? What do they share?*

*Are they honest?
What do they lie about if not?*

---

*How do they view themselves in the
world, do they tend to love or loathe
themselves? Or both?*

*Describe the hardest choice they've ever
had to make…*

---

*What happened one day that
changed everything to them?*

*When was the last time they were
in trouble and what happened?*

---

*How did they cope / what did they
do the day after that happened?*

*What do they think the meaning
of their life is?*

INSIDE-
OUT
STORY
TELLING

INSIDE-OUT STORY-TELLING

An inside-out story lets us know what is happening on the outside of a creature, and also what the creature is experiencing on the inside. For example, lets see what happens to **Oops** here on **Tuesday 4th of May**.

OUTSIDE STORY

Oops went to the post office to post a parcel to his frail beloved grandmother. He waited in line for twenty minutes. By the time he was finally served, his phone rang. It was his grandmother calling and so he answered. He mouthed an apology to the clerk who was helping him, and handed the parcel over as he spoke to his grandmother. The clerk processed the parcel without smiling. Oops passed the clerk the money for the stamp, and then scuttled out of the post office and walked home, all the while listening to his grandmother prattle on about her miserable day.

INSIDE STORY

Oops felt bad that he hadn't seen his grandmother in so long he decided to send her a gift in the mail. When he was at the post office she happened to call him. He answered even though he was about to be served because he was already feeling bad about not seeing her and to not answer her call would have made him feel even worse. He felt so guilty about being on the phone as the clerk processed the parcel. He wondered if the clerk disliked him for being on the phone. He tried to apologise to the clerk so he didn't appear rude but the clerk didn't seem to care. He glanced about wondering if the other people in line thought he was rude as well. He left the post office feeling just as guilty as he did before he sent the parcel.

NOW IT'S YOUR TURN

Write a short story of what happened
to your creature on the outside …

YOUR OUTSIDE STORY

NOW IT'S YOUR TURN

Now write about how they felt on the inside …
How did your creature feel about what happened?
What were they unsure about? What did they think,
but did not say?

YOUR INSIDE STORY

CREATURE INDEX

Clare-Rose Trevelyan
Author

Clare-Rose Trevelyan believes that if all our stories were told, and all of our stories were listened to, we would find ourselves in a more gentle existence.

Her particular love is to get kids thinking about how they are thinking and wondering about why they are wondering, by weaving the questions of eternity through her collections of books.

She collaborates with as many friends as she can, in as many ways as she can, so that the stories end up mirroring a hypnotic, vivid, bouquet of truths.

She likes mysteries and doing absolutely nothing at all with her family and friends, for days and days and days on end.

If you want to stay in touch with Clare, sign up to her newsletter at **www.clare-rose.com**

If you want to buy any of Clare's books go to **www.amazon.com/author/clare_rose**

Yongho Moon
Illustrator

Yongho Moon lived in South Korea before coming to Australia, first to Sydney and then to Melbourne. He has many talents, including skills as an engineer, but his passion is visual contemporary arts and design. His work has been shown both in Australia and South Korea where his media art has been projected on the giant facade of Seoul Square. He loves collaborating with Clare who he says offers him the freedom to develop ideas in his own way.

Francis Lim
Designer

Francis Lim is originally from Singapore. His experience as a designer includes working on many different kinds of publications, company reports, magazine ads, campaigns for State and National organisations such as Museums Victoria. He has been working with Clare for many years, realising her original ideas into beautiful publications, big and small.

ABOUT THE BOOK WITH NO STORY

The Book With No Story is a celebration of diversity in terms of our insides, not our outsides. Our passions, complexities and contradictions. The book weaves in and out of the creatures' worlds, and also their inner emotional landscapes. In it's essence it is an adoration of us all. The kids are asked to create their own characters, venturing into their inside and outside lives, and write them into stories of their own.

If you want to buy *The Book With No Story* go to **www.amazon.com/author/clare_rose**

RED WOOL EDITIONS

Red Wool Editions is a publishing company dedicated to unravelling the philosophical thoughts of kids, by taking them through enchanting stories, twinkling soundtracks and accompanying educational packages for parents and teachers. Our aim is to encourage young readers to create their own stories and open up family discussions on how they want to live their life and why.

If you want to learn about forthcoming publications subscribe to **www.facebook.com/redwooleditions**

THE YOUNG PHILOSOPHERS SERIES

The Young Philosophers Series is intended as a place children can explore philosophy by doing it, rather than by being told about what it is and isn't.

At Red Wool Editions, we believe that children are natural philosophers and so we have started our first series exploring the complexities of oneself, contradiction, the thoughts of others, change, the meaning of life and senses of place. The books focus on the basic elements of storytelling as we venture further into the universe of your thoughts and eventually, your stories.

To find out more about philosophical journaling and other books by Red Wool Editions visit clare-rose.com. You'll also discover our upcoming theme park of activity books that show you how to turn your wonderings into your stories and how those stories may come to both reflect and shape our spellbinding lives.

Young Philosophers

THE BOOK WITH NO STORY
Young Philosophers Series Vol. 1
A Collection of Creatures

Written by Clare-Rose Trevelyan
Illustrator Yongho Moon
Editor Josey De Rossi
Design Futureinform
Photographs by many of our loved ones

Published in 2022 by Red Wool Editions
Copyright © Clare-Rose and Futureinform 2022
All rights reserved.

ISBN 978-1-925864-41-0

Mailing Address
PO BOX 8175 Subiaco East WA 6008

Buy the Books
www.amazon.com/author/clare_rose

What can money not buy you?
How often do you allow yourself
to change your mind about
something?

Is it possible to agree with
two opposing viewpoints?

Do you tend to see the flaws
in others first or the magic?

Do you believe in true love?

Do you forgive yourself easily?